S0-ARP-637

Midlothian
Public Library
14701 S. Kenton Ave.
Midlothian, IL 60445

THE NEED FOR SPEED

RACE CAR LEGENDS

COLLECTOR'S EDITION

A.J. Foyt

The Allisons

Dale Earnhardt Jr.

Danica Patrick

Famous Finishes

Famous Tracks

The Jarretts

Jeff Burton

Jeff Gordon

Jimmie Johnson

Kenny Irwin Jr.

The Labonte Brothers

Lowriders

Mario Andretti

Mark Martin

Monster Trucks & Tractors

Motorcycles

The Need for Speed

Off-Road Racing

The Pit Crew

Rockcrawling

Rusty Wallace

Stunt Driving

Tony Stewart

The Unsers

THE NEED FOR SPEED

Tara Baukus Mello

The Need for Speed

Chelsea House
An imprint of Infobase Publishing
132 West 31st Street
New York NY 10001

ISBN-10: 0-7910-8667-4
ISBN-13: 978-0-7910-8667-4

Library of Congress Cataloging-in-Publication Data
Mello, Tara Baukus.
The need for speed / Tara Baukus Mello.
p. cm. – (Race car legends. Collector's edition)
Includes bibliographical references and index.
ISBN 0-7910-8667-4 (hardcover)
1. Automobile racing drivers—Biography—Juvenile literature. 2. Automobile racing—History—Juvenile literature. I. Title. II. Series.
GV1029.13.M45 2007 796.720922—dc22
[B] 2006035394

Chelsea House books are available at special discounts when purchased in bulk quantities for businesses, associations, institutions, or sales promotions. Please call our Special Sales Department in New York at (212) 967-8800 or (800) 322-8755.

You can find Chelsea House books on the World Wide Web at http://www.chelseahouse.com

Series design by Erika K. Arroyo
Cover design by Hierophant Publishing Services/EON PreMedia/Joo Young An

Printed in the United States of America

Bang PH 10 9 8 7 6 5 4 3 2 1

This book is printed on acid-free paper.

All links and Web addresses were checked and verified to be correct at the time of publication. Because of the dynamic nature of the Web, some addresses and links may have changed since publication and may no longer be valid.

CONTENTS

1

FASTER THAN THE SPEED OF SOUND

Nevada's Black Rock Desert is a vast, isolated place where a visitor can look in every direction and see nothing for miles but flat, hard, sun-baked sand with dark mountains in the distance. It is so big that a visitor can start at the south end of Black Rock and drive at highway speeds for an hour and still not reach the other end. The stretch of sand, 86 miles long and 20 miles wide, is actually a dry lakebed that is 1.5 billion years old. The hot temperatures and dry air of the desert climate have turned the once-sandy surface to a hard crust, as though it had been fired in a kiln like a ceramic pot.

Each year, the desert floor floods with a few inches of rain. Strong winds sweep across the water, blowing it and any loose sand grains into the cracks and crevices on the desert floor. As temperatures climb, the water evaporates, and the dry surface becomes one of the longest, smoothest, and flattest places in the world.

The *Thrust SSC's* camp in the Black Rock Desert near Gerlach, Nevada, is dwarfed against an expanse of the ancient lakebed that was used as the proving ground for breaking the land speed record during the autumn of 1997.

Early one morning in October 1997, a cloud of dust could be seen rising from the desert floor. In front of that cloud was an immense black vehicle that looked a bit like a giant set of binoculars. The huge car shimmered as it sped across the desert landscape and seemed almost to be hovering over the ground.

A moment later, a muffled boom came from the car, and the Black Rock Desert once again went down in history. That shiny black car had just broken the **sound barrier**. It was the first time that a vehicle had traveled fast enough

THE SOUND OF THUNDER

When any vehicle approaches the speed of sound, shock waves are formed. These shock waves are the buildup of sound waves, which can only travel through the air at the speed of sound. When an airplane travels faster than the speed of sound, it pushes on the sound waves, causing them to pile up against each other, creating shock waves. If you are on the ground below the plane when this happens, the sound waves enter your ear and make your eardrum vibrate. Your brain interprets these vibrations as a "sonic boom."

For example, when a space shuttle reenters Earth's atmosphere, it creates a sonic boom. But other, more common things can create a sonic boom, too. Probably the best-known sonic boom happens during a storm. When lightning strikes, it heats the air and causes shock waves. These shock waves cause sonic booms, otherwise known as thunder.

on land to achieve this feat, but it wasn't the first time the Black Rock Desert had made land speed racing history.

A British man named Richard Noble made the Black Rock Desert famous in 1983 when he set a world land speed record there. Since the 1930s, the Bonneville Salt Flats in Utah, located 600 miles east of Black Rock, had been the most commonly used location for attempts at a world land speed record. The salt flats, along with a few other places, were the only spots in the world where a person who wanted to be the "fastest on Earth" could safely attempt to set a land speed record.

The Bonneville Salt Flats, however, were deteriorating. The dried salt on the lakebed, which had been Lake

The *Thrust SSC*, driven by British Royal Air Force pilot Andy Green, speeds along at 763.035 miles per hour during the first leg of its record-breaking land speed run on October 15, 1997.

Bonneville billions of years ago, had gone from being several feet thick to just a few inches thick in spots. The size of the area suitable for racing was also shrinking. Yet, as record speeds increased, the teams needed more room.

THE RIVALS

In 1982, Richard Noble and his *Thrust 2* team traveled from Great Britain to the United States, where they would try to set a land speed record at the Bonneville Salt Flats. Although British teams had held many records in the early years of the sport, Americans had consistently been the record setters since 1964. An American racer named

Craig Breedlove, who was the first person to travel 400, 500, and 600 miles per hour (mph) in a car, led the way. When Noble arrived at Bonneville, he hoped to break the American streak of record making. But an unusual rainstorm submerged the racetrack in a few inches of water, making racing there unsafe. In search of another location, Noble found the Black Rock Desert, but it wasn't until he returned the following year that he broke Gary Gabelich's 13-year-old record and made the desert famous in the world of land speed racing.

As hard as Breedlove and others tried, no one was able to break Noble's record of 633.470 mph. At times, different teams, including Breedlove's *Spirit of America*, traveled faster than the *Thrust 2* without officially breaking the record. The rules of land speed racing require two runs to be made on the same course, in opposite directions, less than one hour apart. The speeds from the two runs are averaged together to get one speed, and only that number is the official speed.

As the years passed, two strong contenders emerged: Noble and Breedlove. When they arrived in the Black Rock Desert in 1997, the two men began a competition that became known as the "Duel in the Desert." Noble was by this time the head of the *Thrust SSC* team (SSC stood for "**supersonic** car") and had chosen British Royal Air Force pilot Andy Green as his driver. Breedlove led the *Spirit of America-Sonic Arrow* team and was also the car's driver. Everything about the two cars was different—their size, their shape, their color, and even the type of fuel they used. But most people thought that both teams had cars capable of setting a new record. The competition was going to be tough.

The *Spirit of America-Sonic Arrow* and *Thrust SSC* teams were sharing Black Rock Desert, each team taking turns at making passes across the vast sand that was their racetrack. *Thrust SSC* first broke the sound barrier on October 13. The dust cloud that trailed behind the car hung for a moment, suspended in the air, and then dropped suddenly as the car broke through the sound barrier with a muffled boom. As the *Thrust SSC*'s **aerodynamics** expert expected, the desert floor absorbed most of the sound, leaving only a muted noise. Usually, a loud, ear-popping sound is made when a plane breaks through the sound barrier in the air.

It may have been relatively quiet at the Black Rock Desert when Andy Green broke the sound barrier, but the people in the town of Gerlach, 15 miles away, were startled when the booming noise shook the ground. It caused bottles to bounce around and dishes to move, and even knocked some ceiling tiles loose at the local school. Some of the people in the town said it felt like an earthquake.

Although the noise was not overwhelming to those who stood in the desert watching the *Thrust SSC* speed across the sand, the sight of Green breaking through the sound barrier was spectacular. Those watching saw the air build up in front of the car in the form of **shock waves**. Later, when spectators walked out to the spot where Green had traveled at supersonic speeds, they saw something incredible. The tracks that led up to the point where he broke the sound barrier looked much like normal tire tracks. But where Green had begun traveling at supersonic speeds, the tracks became deep ruts, as if a farmer had torn through the desert with a plow.

Up until that day, no one was really sure if the sound barrier could ever be safely broken on land. Chuck

Yeager, a U.S. Air Force captain, was the first person to break the sound barrier with an airplane in October 1947. Before that day, people thought that an airplane would break apart as it reached the sound barrier. A vehicle would have to go much faster on land than in the air because the speed of sound is directly linked to temperature. When Yeager broke the sound barrier, he traveled at 670 mph in a rocket-powered Bell X-1 airplane. Even if the temperature were just 30°F (1°C), a vehicle on land would need to travel at 739 mph to reach the speed of sound.

Chuck Yeager, one of the greatest test pilots in history and the first pilot to break the sound barrier, is shown in 1985 standing in front of the rocket-powered Bell X-1E plane that he flew faster than the speed of sound in 1947.

Andy Green (*left*) and Richard Noble hoist Britain's flag in celebration of beating the land speed record on October 15, 1997.

To travel that fast, a person would first need to build a car that could both reach those speeds and withstand the forces of the sound waves hitting it without being damaged. Then a driver would need to find a location where he or she could safely reach that speed and still have enough room to bring the car to a stop. When the *Thrust SSC* team put all these factors together, they went down in the record books.

THE BRITISH TAKE THE LEAD

Although Green made history on October 13, 1997, when he broke the sound barrier on land, it wasn't until October 15 that he set the current world land speed record. Green made two runs on October 13, one at 760 mph and the other at 763 mph, but it took him 61 minutes to complete both runs. This was just one minute longer than the rules allowed. So, to set an official record, he had to try again. Two days later, the *Thrust SSC* team set the official record with two runs averaging 763.035 mph.

The day was a huge victory for the British, but it was a crushing defeat for Breedlove and his *Spirit of America* team. When Breedlove arrived at Black Rock that summer, he didn't expect the *Thrust SSC* team to set the record at 763 mph, up from the previous record of 633 mph. It was a huge jump, and one for which the American team hadn't been prepared. Among other problems, the *Spirit of America-Sonic Arrow*'s wheels were only guaranteed for speeds of up to 650 mph. This was good enough to break Noble's 1983 record but not good enough to travel at supersonic speeds.

Today, a few teams are still working to break Green's world record, but so far, no one has come close to the speed of sound since that October day.

2

THE HISTORY OF LAND SPEED RACING

For more than 100 years, people have felt the need for speed. The first land speed record was set in 1898, just a short time after the automobile itself was invented. The quest for reaching the fastest speed on land began in Europe, where two men—one from France and one from Belgium—each wanted to be known as the "fastest man on Earth." To make his attempt, Count Gaston de Chasseloup-Laubat arranged for a special timed run on an open road in Archeres, France. On December 18, 1898, he drove his car, a Jeantaud, at a record speed of 39.24 mph. By today's standards, the speed was not very fast. But for that time, it was an amazing speed because the count's car had just one tiny electric motor that put out about 36 horsepower. Horsepower is a measurement of the power of an engine. Typical cars on the road today run on engines of 120 to more than 450 horsepower.

The count's rival in his record-setting quest was Camille Janatzy, from Belgium. Janatzy could not make it to France on December 18, so he challenged the count to another race. On January 17, 1899, the two men competed, and both of them broke the count's earlier record. They then raced each other during the course of several months, each trying to make his car go the fastest.

Land speed racing had been around for only a few months, and already there was serious competition. Then, one day in April 1899, Janatzy arrived with an electric car he had specially designed to break the record. The car, named *La Jamais Contente* ("the Never Satisfied"), set a record of 65.79 mph. Three years went by before Janatzy's record was broken.

As the automobile was being developed, cars that ran on gasoline and steam were improved, and fewer electric vehicles were produced. In one of the new steam-powered cars, Leon Serpollet of France broke Janatzy's record, reaching speeds of 75.06 mph along the seaside in Nice, France. The speed was so fast that Serpollet said the only way he could breathe was by turning his head to the side while he was driving.

THE TAKEOVER OF THE GAS ENGINE

But steam-powered engines would never become popular in the world of car building. Steam cars were neither intended to be the transportation of choice, nor destined to hold records for speed. Soon the gasoline-powered engine took over, and it seemed that people all over the world were trying to use it to set a land speed record. The French and the Belgians were still involved, as was an Englishman named Charles Rolls, who later began the Rolls-Royce Motor Company.

Henry Ford stands beside his race car with race car driver Barney Oldfield. In 1904, Ford drove this four-cylinder, 80 horsepower car to a world speed record of 91.4 miles per hour on the ice of Lake St. Clair, Michigan.

In the United States, Henry Ford, founder of the Ford Motor Company, thought that land speed racing might be a good way to get some publicity for his new company. He built a car called the Arrow with a four-cylinder engine that produced 70 horsepower. In January 1904, he drove it at 91.37 mph on a frozen lake in Michigan. A few days later, American millionaire William Vanderbilt Jr. set a new record in a Mercedes Simplex. Vanderbilt drove at 92.30 mph on the sand at Daytona Beach in Florida. Daytona Beach became a popular place for Americans to

BREAKING THE 100 BARRIER

The first person to drive faster than 100 mph was Frenchman Louis Rigolly, driving a Gobron-Brillie. In the city of Ostend, in Belgium, Rigolly set the record at 103.55 mph on July 21, 1904. But his record would not last long. By the end of the year, a man named Victor Hemery broke Rigolly's record driving a Darracq powered by an early form of the V-8 engine.

race. Although there is no racing on the sand there today, it is one of the few places where a car can legally be driven on the beach.

The meeting to race on the beach at Daytona became known as Florida Speed Week. Twin brothers Francis Edgar Stanley and Freelan Oscar Stanley—commonly called F.E. and F.O. for short—built a steam car, the Rocket, to race against the gasoline-powered cars. In 1906, their driver Fred Marriott easily topped the speed of the gasoline cars with a run of 121.57 mph. A year later, Marriott also had the first crash in land speed racing history. It was amazing that he survived.

The last time a land speed record was set on a public road was in 1924, near Paris, France. That record speed clocked in at 146.01 mph.

In the 1920s, Malcolm Campbell, a racer at England's Brooklands and a former British Royal Flying Corps captain, became one of the main people involved in land speed racing. He called his blue-painted car the *Bluebird*, and various versions of it competed for the record for many years. Campbell broke the record in 1925 by setting a speed of 150.766 mph.

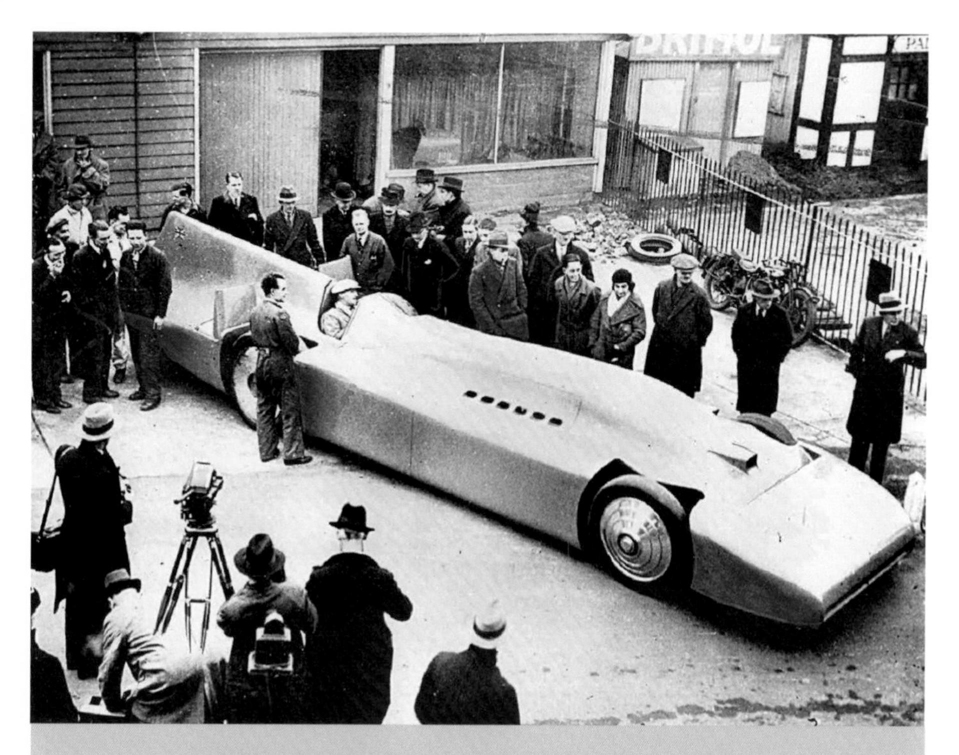

British race car driver Malcolm Campbell sits in the cockpit of the *Bluebird V* shortly before it was shipped to the United States for its attempt to win back the land speed record in 1935. Campbell went on to set the record at 301.129 miles per hour at the Bonneville Salt Flats in Utah.

FRENCH VS. AMERICAN

In the early days of land speed racing, the French Automobile Club (AFC) oversaw the timing of world record attempts and made them official. By 1911, the AFC decided that to be official, all new records had to be the average of two runs in opposite directions over the same racecourse. This rule is still used today. The first two-way record was set at the Brooklands track in England in 1914, where L.G. Hornstead drove at 124.10 mph. American racers, however, didn't want to follow this new rule and kept setting their own one-way records, which they called the "American record."

One of the *Bluebird*'s main competitors was the *Sunbeam*, driven by Major Henry Seagrave. Louis Coatalen designed the vehicle, which had two engines that together produced less than 1,000 horsepower. It was thought that this car could travel at 200 mph. The British Sunbeam team traveled to Daytona, where the beach was long enough to try to set a new record. In March 1927, tens of thousands of people lined the beach to watch the *Sunbeam* make its first run in the United States. Major Seagrave set the new record, traveling an average of 203.792 mph during his two passes on the sand.

The *Blue Flame*, driven by Gary Gabelich, performs a test run at the Bonneville Salt Flats in Utah before setting the new land speed record at 622.407 miles per hour in October 1970.

Two years later, in March 1929, he raced in a new vehicle called the *Golden Arrow*. With 100,000 people watching, Seagrave set a record speed of 231.446 mph.

In the early 1930s, Campbell won back the land speed record and decided that his next goal would be to reach 300 mph. The beach at Daytona, however, was too soft and bumpy to drive at that speed. Campbell needed to find another place to race. He chose the Bonneville Salt Flats in Utah, a giant dry lakebed made of solid salt. In 1935, Campbell set his last land speed record there, driving a new *Bluebird* at 301.129 mph.

FASTER AND FASTER

By the 1940s, land speed racers were aiming for 400 mph. An English racer named John Cobb was by this time involved in the sport. He set a new record in 1947 of 394.196 mph, just narrowly missing the 400-mph mark.

Cobb's record stood until 1963, when Craig Breedlove claimed the record driving the *Spirit of America*. But the governing race organization, the Fédération International de l'Automobile (FIA), said Breedlove's record wasn't official. The rules said that the car had to have four wheels and be powered by two of them. The *Spirit of America* was in fact powered by a jet engine. So many people had built jet-engine cars for land speed racing that the FIA created a new category.

In 1964, many teams went to Bonneville with jet cars to try to erase the record. Breedlove set the record at 468.72 mph but knew he could go faster. He did: A few days later, he reached 526.28 mph. But on the return run, he lost control and crashed into a small lake at the end of the course. Fortunately, Breedlove was unhurt. He and his

Members of the "600 MPH Club": (*from left*) Richard Noble, Craig Breedlove, Andy Green, and Art Arfons gather together by the Gerlach, Nevada, city limits sign.

team worked hard to build a new car, the *Spirit of America-Sonic I*, which he raced the following year. After breaking the 400 mph and 500 mph barriers, Breedlove went on to speed through the 600-mph barrier at 600.601 mph in November 1965.

In 1970, driver Gary Gabelich set the record at 622.407 mph, driving a car called the *Blue Flame* that was powered by a liquid-fuel rocket engine. Gabelich's record stood until 1983. It was then that Richard Noble arrived on the scene with the *Thrust 2*, beginning a new competition between the British and the Americans in their quest to drive the fastest car on Earth.

3

THE *SPIRIT OF AMERICA*

My ninth birthday was a monumental occasion, for which I impatiently waited. I got my first bicycle and, with it, the obsession for speed that has remained with me ever since. I gleefully wheeled the bike down the front porch steps that morning and out onto the sidewalk in search of the neighborhood kids—not to show off the gleaming chrome or the white sidewall tires, but to show them how fast it would go.

—Craig Breedlove in his book, *Spirit of America*

Breedlove knows all about the need for speed. His ninth birthday, on March 23, 1946, may have been the first time he longed to show the world how fast he could go, but it certainly wasn't his last time. For the man who was the first person to travel 400, 500, and 600 mph on land, going fast became his work and his hobby.

He bought his first car, a 1934 Ford coupe, when he was just 13. After spending three years modifying it into a **hot rod**, he won his first auto race in it at age 16. By the time he was 21, Breedlove had built a car that he raced at 236 mph at the Bonneville Salt Flats. Just one year later,

Craig Breedlove is lifted into the air by his crew after becoming the first man to break the 600-mile-per-hour land speed barrier in 1965.

he began to follow his dream of building a vehicle that would set the world land speed record. The first *Spirit of America* was born, and, in 1963, Breedlove drove it to a record 407 mph. With that accomplishment also came the honor of being the first American to hold the land speed record in more than 32 years.

With drag racing growing in popularity in the United States, Breedlove was suddenly competing with other Americans for the title of fastest man on Earth. During the next two years, he raced his *Spirit of America* many times in an effort to keep the title. On one run in October 1964, Breedlove lost his parachutes and his brakes. Unable to stop the car, he went wildly off the course, crashing through

BREEDLOVE AND THE BEACH BOYS

Craig Breedlove's racing efforts made him a celebrity in the United States. People nicknamed him "Captain America." The 1960s rock group the Beach Boys even wrote about him in their song "Little Deuce Coupe." They sang:

An airplane, an auto now famous worldwide
Spirit of America, the name on the side
The man who would drive her, Craig Breedlove by name
A daring young man played a dangerous game.

some telephone poles at 400 mph and snapping them like twigs. The car stopped only when it ran into a small salt pond, where it quickly sank. Breedlove was unhurt and swam to safety. Amazingly, he had gone through the timing lights, so his wild ride counted, and he logged a new record at 526.277 mph.

Even though he had just experienced a very serious crash, Breedlove and his team started building a new car right away. The new one, the *Spirit of America-Sonic I*, had a J-79 jet engine. In another daring move, he became the first man to reach 600 mph on land, which set a new record in 1965. This record wasn't broken until 1970, and it marked the last time that Breedlove was the fastest man on Earth.

Although his last record was in 1965, Breedlove's need for speed has never slowed. In fact, it may have made his desire stronger. After experimenting with a rocket dragster in the 1970s and 1980s, Breedlove began building the *Spirit of America-Sonic Arrow* in 1992 to try to recapture the world land speed record for the United States. It was

Craig Breedlove sets his last ground speed record of 600.601 miles per hour in the *Spirit of America* at the Bonneville Salt Flats in 1965.

this car that became the challenger to Richard Noble's *Thrust SSC* in the 1997 showdown at the Black Rock Desert in Nevada.

OBSTACLES IN THE COURSE

In 1996, the newest *Spirit of America* was ready to run, but it met problems on the way. Breedlove and the team went to the Black Rock Desert, hoping to set a new world record.

When they arrived, a group of environmental protesters tried to stop them from racing because the group felt that racing such a big and powerful vehicle at such high speeds would be damaging to the desert environment. Breedlove and his team had all the proper permits from the Bureau of Land Management, which oversaw the Black Rock Desert, but it took a judge six weeks to decide that the *Spirit of America* could race on the desert that year. Finally, on October 28, Breedlove was able to make a run, but a series of misunderstandings led to disaster.

First, the distance Breedlove needed to reach his goal speed before hitting the timing lights had been poorly calculated. As a result, when he passed through the timing lights he was traveling much faster than he had planned. In addition, he had misunderstood the wind report from farther up the course. The voice over the team's two-way radio told him "one five," which he thought meant 1.5 knots, or about 2 miles per hour. This would have been perfectly safe for making a run. But the wind was actually gusting at 15 knots, or about 17 miles per hour—far too windy to safely control the vehicle.

Once Breedlove realized there was something wrong, he made the quick decision to kill the power to the engine. The sudden change caused the *Spirit of America* to become unstable. Combined with the terrible winds, this caused the car to go completely out of control. It began moving in a giant U-turn, eventually rolling up on its left side and sliding until it finally lost enough speed to drop back on all its wheels. When the car finally stopped, Breedlove was uninjured, but the *Spirit of America* was beyond quick repair. It looked as if 1996 would not be the year for Breedlove to set a new record.

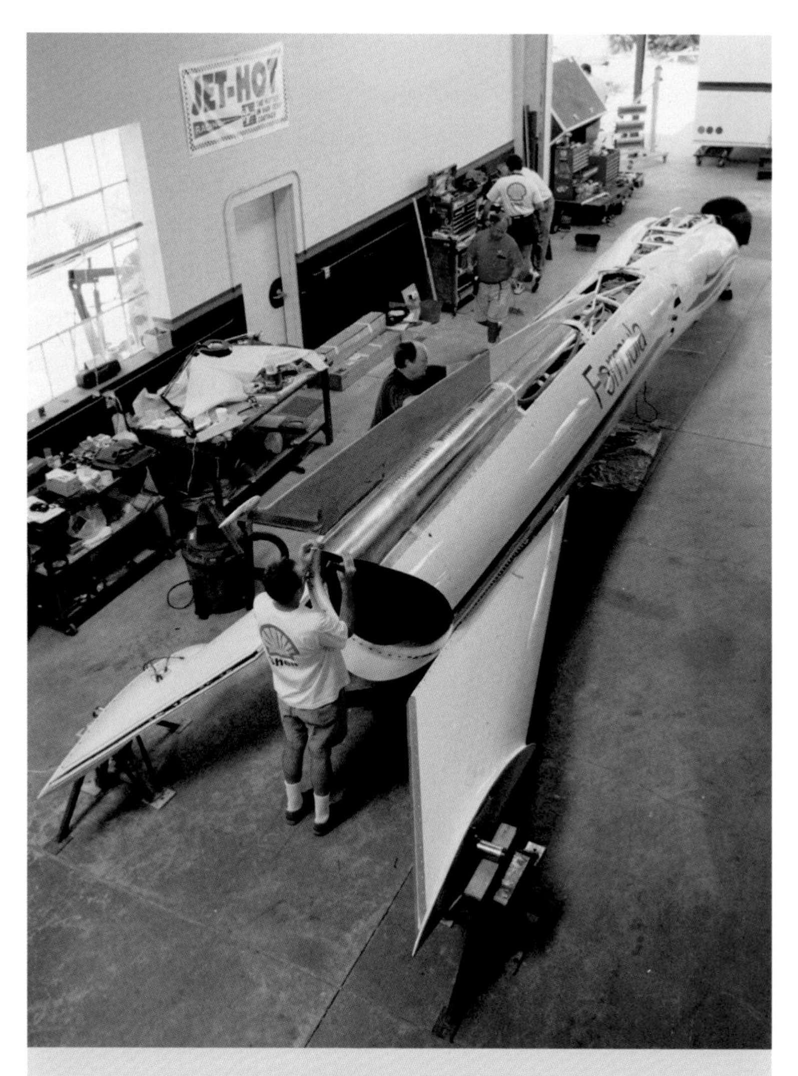

Crewmembers work on the jet-powered *Spirit of America* in Craig Breedlove's garage in preparation for the showdown with Richard Noble's *Thrust SSC* in 1997.

THE SPIRIT MOVES ON

The 1996 *Spirit of America* had a jet engine just like the one with which Breedlove had set records in the 1960s, with one exception. To get the gasoline company Shell as a team sponsor, he converted the car to run on the kind of gasoline that a person would put in a normal passenger car. The engine produced 45,000 horsepower and was located at the rear of the vehicle. The cockpit where Breedlove sat was located in the front, and the steering was similar to that of an airplane. To stop the *Spirit of America*, there were two parachutes and special brakes on all four wheels. There was also something that Breedlove described as his "Fred Flintstone brake"—actually a ski that dropped from the car's nose to the ground and that could slow the car from 60 mph to a stop in one to three miles. It was the last brake in the series that Breedlove used to stop his car.

When the *Spirit of America* met the *Thrust SSC* at the Black Rock Desert in 1997, everyone had high hopes that Breedlove could break Richard Noble's 1983 record of 633.470 mph. But the *Spirit of America*'s problems began almost immediately. Its engine was badly damaged on the third run, and the team was forced to return to their shop in California to get the spare engine. By the time the new engine was ready for another run, the *Thrust SSC* team had already set a new record at 714 mph.

Before it even had a chance to get back into the game, the *Spirit of America* was out again: Its wheels could travel safely only at 700 mph or slower. Breedlove and the team tried their best to make a competitive run just the same, but the replacement engine never performed as well as the first engine had. Then the *Thrust SSC* team broke the sound barrier and set a new record at 763.035 mph.

It was almost a full month before the *Spirit of America* was ready to run again, with wheels safe for up to 800 mph. But by this time, winter was closing in, and the seasonal rains had begun. The *Spirit of America* could not run without becoming bogged down in the desert sand, which had

The *Spirit of America* creates a cloud of dust as it travels 227 miles per hour during its first test run on the sun-baked surface of the Black Rock Desert in September 1997.

loosened with the rain. On November 17, 1997, the team packed up its equipment and headed home.

The team hoped to race again in 1998 but couldn't raise enough money to cover the costs. Shell, the primary sponsor the year before, was going through major business changes and wasn't able to participate. In 1999, Breedlove learned he needed to have surgery to repair his shoulder, which he had hurt when he fell while jogging. Although he held on to hope, he was never able to reach his goal of building a new car able to travel faster than 800 mph. He has not made a land speed record attempt since.

4

THE *THRUST SSC*

When Richard Noble set the world land speed record in 1983 at the Black Rock Desert, it was an accomplishment for which he worked very hard. For three years in a row, Noble had taken the *Thrust 2* to the United States to race, only to go back to England without setting a record. When he finally did set the land speed record, it was 11 mph faster than the previous record. This was just a tiny bit faster than what racing officials required for a new record. Rules state that a new record must be at least one percent faster than the old record. Noble was the fastest man on Earth, but just barely.

He immediately began to make plans for a new land speed record, and the next goal that made sense to him was 700 mph. Noble also knew that the speed of sound was just beyond that, at about 740 mph. No one had ever before broken the sound barrier in a car. Noble's sponsors were not ready to provide the necessary funds, though, so he moved on to new projects.

Noble started a company that built inexpensive, lightweight airplanes and also worked on a boat that he hoped would break the speed record for crossing the Atlantic Ocean. In 1990, he encountered Craig Breedlove at the

Richard Noble drives the *Thrust 2* while a Spitfire aircraft flies overhead during an air show in England in 1980. Exhibiting the various versions of the *Thrust* to the public over the years was one way Noble raised funds for the program.

Bonneville Salt Flats and learned that Breedlove was working on a plan to break Noble's land speed record. Noble took it as a challenge and once again began to think about land speed racing and breaking the sound barrier with a car.

A DREAM COME TRUE

Two years passed, but the idea remained in Noble's head. His ideas become a reality when he met Ron Ayers, a man who had the experience to help design a car that could travel safely at supersonic speeds. Ayers started to work on the design for the car that would be named the *Thrust SSC*. Meanwhile, Noble began putting together a team and raising money to fund the very expensive process of building, testing, and racing the car. In addition to the companies that provided funding and parts for the project, individuals contributed money through the **Mach 1** Club. A Web site for the *Thrust SSC* was also designed, which featured regular updates and photos. It was another way for the team to raise additional funds and get new members in the Mach 1 Club.

The *Thrust SSC* began taking shape. The team determined that, if all went well, they could have the car completed in about two years—the spring of 1996. In the meantime, both Noble and Breedlove agreed to meet at the Black Rock Desert in a showdown to see whether the Americans could reclaim the record or whether the Brits could surpass Noble's 1983 speed. The two met in California and worked out an agreement in which they would share the desert racetrack.

Testing their cars was very important to both teams because they needed to be sure about their capabilities when it came time to meet at Black Rock. Noble's team chose the Al Jafr Desert in Jordan for its testing grounds. In June 1996, the *Thrust SSC* team had planned to take the car to the Jordanian desert for testing, but it was nowhere near complete, and money was running low. Instead, they displayed the car at the Goodwood Festival of Speed, a famous and historic race in England. It was at this event that many people saw Noble's new car for the first time. Money from the purchase of *Thrust SSC* merchandise and donations from Mach 1 Club members helped fill the team's bank account.

The team worked day and night for the next few months, until the car was completed in August. Before the *Thrust SSC* was transported to the desert, it was tested on an airport runway in England. When the car moved on its own for the first time, the team discovered that its brakes were so powerful that the front tires actually burst.

At the same time as the Noble team's arrival in Jordan, Breedlove was testing the *Spirit of America* on the other

Andy Green deploys a chute to slow down the *Thrust SSC* during a speed trial at the Farnborough airfield in Hampshire, England, in October 1996.

side of the world. As the British team began to prepare for its first runs, word came that Breedlove had had an accident while making a giant U-turn at high speed. Although they knew that he was not hurt, everyone on the British team was reminded of the dangers of their projects. After problems with the steering and bad weather, the *Thrust SSC* team was forced to abandon their racing for the year, just as Breedlove had done. The *Thrust SSC* had only traveled up to 331 mph in the Al Jafr Desert.

The winter of 1996 was spent redesigning and rebuilding the *Thrust SSC*, and plans were made to return to the Al Jafr Desert in the spring of 1997 for more testing. Fundraising, which continued as the costs of the project grew, became increasingly difficult. It was hard to convince companies to sponsor a car that could break the sound barrier when the team hadn't even proved it was capable of going half that speed. The team did some low-speed testing of the new and improved *Thrust SSC* on an airport runway in England. After the testing, they decided they were ready to go back to Jordan that May.

REDEFINING THE DESERT

Jordan's Al Jafr Desert was not the ideal place to test the *Thrust SSC*. Although the Jordanian government and military were very helpful to the team, the country's landscape was a problem. Dips in the surface needed to be smoothed, an access road for the team's large trucks needed to be built, and thousands of stones that littered the desert had to be collected. Some members of the team went to Jordan early to prepare the site.

Only a few months remained before the competition with Breedlove at Black Rock. The British team spent just over two weeks at Al Jafr and got the car up to 540 mph. Then they returned to England to make the final preparations, putting the car on a Russian cargo ship and transporting it to the United States.

FINDING FUNDING

The team's biggest challenge, however, was not getting the car ready for its world record attempt. The challenge was raising enough money to get the car to Black Rock for racing. The total cost for the *Thrust SSC* project was about $8 million. It cost $250,000 just for the fuel for the cargo ship to carry the car to the United States.

When the *Thrust SSC* team returned to England that spring, Noble told the crewmembers that they needed to raise about $1 million more to race at Black Rock. The team organized "open days" for Mach 1 Club members and people who belonged to car clubs in England to view the *Thrust SSC.* The team sold team merchandise at these events and on the team Web site. Although they raised some money, it was not enough.

When journalists arrived for an event specially organized for them, they were told that it would be the last time people would see the *Thrust SSC* unless more money came in. With help from the media, donations began to arrive in full force. The Mach 1 Club was not going to let the team get so close to its goal and then not go to Black Rock. Although the team didn't raise the full amount they needed, they raised enough to get the team going again and to convince some companies to join in sponsorship.

A VERY UNUSUAL CAR

After all the redesigning and revising that had taken place since the car was first tested the year before, the jet-black *Thrust SSC* that arrived in the Black Rock Desert was 54 feet long, 12 feet wide, and weighed 10.5 tons when fully fueled. Driver Andy Green sat in the tiny cockpit, right between the two giant Rolls-Royce Spey airplane engines. Together, the engines produced 110,000 horsepower, about the same amount of power as 850 of today's Honda Civics combined.

The arrow-shaped center section of the car—designed with aerodynamics in mind, to help keep the car on the ground—made the *Thrust SSC* look a bit like a set of giant black binoculars held up to the face of a person with a very pointy nose. The front of the car's body was made out of carbon fiber to help reduce weight. The center of the body was made of aluminum to serve as extra protection from the engine heat. Titanium was used for the rear part of the car's body because it is a strong metal that isn't affected by the tremendous shock waves that occur when such a car is traveling at high speeds. The chassis—the frame on which a car's body is placed—was made out of very strong steel tubing. Four wheels, all 34 inches in diameter, were made out of solid aluminum and did not have any rubber tires.

Perhaps the *Thrust SSC*'s most unusual feature was its rear-wheel steering. Only a few types of vehicles are steered with their rear wheels, including shopping carts, forklifts, and dump trucks. Today's cars all steer with their front wheels, but there simply wasn't enough room around the *Thrust SSC*'s front wheels to allow them to steer the car. In addition, the front wheels, located right under the

Andy Green dons his helmet as he enters the tiny cockpit of the *Thrust SSC*.

Rolls-Royce engines, needed to support more than half the weight of the car, which meant that they already had a large and very important job to do.

To test out the idea of rear-wheel steering, the team modified a tiny British car called a Mini and drove it on a test track in England. The little car had its rear wheels removed and an odd-looking contraption resembling

The *Thrust SSC*, looking very much like a pointy nose emerging from a pair of binoculars, rests on the packed sand of the Black Rock Desert after breaking the sound barrier.

a trailer attached. The wheels on the trailerlike device were the ones used to steer the car. Deciding on rear-wheel steering for the *Thrust SSC* was perhaps one of the most radical things the team tried. It meant that driver Andy Green had to relearn how to drive because this new version of the car was so different from the old one. But after much testing, the team decided that their unusual Mini was easier to drive in a straight line and easier to control when cornering than a conventional Mini. This made them confident that the steering would work for the *Thrust SSC*. It was a very unusual car, indeed!

5

SCIENCE AND SAFETY

Driving at speeds fast enough to break the world land speed record requires more than just hopping in the driver's seat, buckling up the seat belt, and pressing the accelerator pedal to the floor. It requires not only a driver with the skills to control a vehicle at high speeds, but also behind-the-scenes people who can determine how to safely make the vehicle go that fast. When driver Andy Green traveled faster than the speed of sound in 1997, it was after years of conducting tests and analyzing scientific data.

Ron Ayers, the chief specialist in aerodynamics for a large company in Britain, met Richard Noble in 1992. When they met, Noble told Ayers about his dream of building a car that would not only set a new land speed record, but also travel at supersonic speeds. "My immediate reaction was to distance myself from the project," Ayers said. "To drive at supersonic speeds would clearly be extremely dangerous, and indeed, it could well be impossible. . . . The aerodynamic forces would simply be enormous—quite enough to lift the car and throw it around like an autumn leaf in a gale."

Richard Noble waves from behind the wheel of the partially completed *Thrust 2* on display in England in 1980. The steel roll cage, constructed for safety purposes, is visible. Noble set the land speed record in this vehicle, powered by a single Rolls-Royce jet engine, in 1983. The *Thrust SSC* features twin jet engines to increase stability and speed.

Although Ayers had serious concerns about the project at the beginning, Noble's question—what the best shape for a supersonic car would be—began to occupy Ayer's mind. Soon, he began thinking about the greatest challenges he would face in building a car that could travel faster than the speed of sound.

Keeping the car stable and on the ground at such high speeds was Ayer's greatest concern. He thought that having a vehicle with an engine on each side made the most sense because the weight and the power would be spread out equally. He believed that a Rolls-Royce Spey engine, which was used in the British version of the Phantom fighter jet, was a good choice because of its power and reliability. But this kind of engine also weighed a lot, which meant that the supersonic car would be very large and extremely heavy.

Ayers talked with Noble and soon created a sketch of his idea for the best shape for the car. Ayers described it as "a twin-jet fighter with the wings removed." Although Ayers was very knowledgeable about aerodynamics, no one really had any idea whether the car he designed could be built to travel safely at faster than 700 mph. Ayers and Noble needed to perform many complicated tests before they built the car, and then they needed to do more testing on the car itself.

To test the aerodynamics on land vehicles, engineers often use a **wind tunnel**. This tool is literally a tunnel with giant fans that move the air around a car at a certain speed. When a vehicle is placed in the tunnel, engineers study how the air flows around the car. Then they change the shape of the car's body to help make it more stable.

One of the simple things that makes a car more stable is a wing on the rear or trunk area of the car. Race cars often have these wings, as do some regular passenger cars. A rear wing guides the air moving across the top of the vehicle and causes the air to push on the rear end of the car. The effect is similar to what would happen if a very strong person pushed down on the rear of the vehicle. This is called **downforce**.

A wind tunnel measures the air that travels underneath the vehicle, too. This air movement is also an important factor in aerodynamics. The air under a vehicle pushes up on the underside of the car as it flows out the sides and back of the car. At high speeds, the force of the air can be so great that it causes the car to rise off the ground and sometimes flip over. Passenger cars don't usually travel fast enough for this to happen, but it sometimes happens to race cars.

A smoke trail illustrates how air flows over a car during a demonstration in a wind tunnel at an aerodynamics lab.

As land speed racers built cars to travel faster and faster, the movement of the air above, around, and underneath the vehicle became more important. Good aerodynamics could mean the difference between reaching the desired speed and crashing. It was not possible for a wind tunnel to simulate the aerodynamic forces at supersonic speeds. So, the *Thrust SSC* team began looking for other ways to test whether the car Ayers designed would work.

Ayers learned that the airflow around the car could be studied using a process called computational fluid dynamics (CFD). This is a complex process that simulates airflow and is performed by a very powerful computer. Each test using CFD took the team's computer six hours to complete. Once the CFD tests were complete, the *Thrust SSC* team knew that Ayer's basic design could be used. This was only the beginning of testing, though. Next, they built a scale model of the vehicle and performed tests on a **rocket sled**. When the rockets attached to the sled were fired, the sled's speed rapidly increased.

This wasn't the first time that testing was done with rocket sleds. The U.S. military has been using the method for many years. In one test in 1954, a U.S. Air Force colonel strapped himself to a rocket sled and traveled at a then-record speed of 632 mph. When the nine rockets that powered the sled were fired, it took just five seconds for the sled to speed down a 35,000-foot track. During that same series of tests, other, unmanned, rocket sleds traveled at speeds as fast as 2,850 mph. The rocket sled testing that the *Thrust SSC* performed involved 13 different tries, with the scale model of the car traveling as fast as 820 mph.

A rocket sled sits on the high-speed test track at Holloman Air Force Base, New Mexico. A scale model of the *Thrust SSC* was tested on a rocket sled as part of the design process.

WHAT IS THE WORST THAT COULD HAPPEN?

Although all the tests indicated that a car could travel at supersonic speed, no one could really be sure what would happen when the *Thrust SSC* team tried to do so with their vehicle. What was most important to Noble, Ayers, and the rest of the team was the safety of the driver, Andy Green. There was the possibility that the nose of the *Thrust SSC* would lift as Green approached the speed of sound and that the car would roll over or spin out of control. The team needed to create not only a car that they believed would safely reach that speed, but also a car that would ensure Green's safety in the worst possible accident they could imagine.

Like all race cars, the *Thrust SSC* had a steel roll cage and special straps, called driver restraints, to make sure Green's arms didn't fly around in the event that he lost control. But these features, which protect a race car driver in most cases, don't necessarily work very well if the race car goes out of control at a very high speed. The key to keeping Green safe was to make sure the car didn't go out of control. The *Thrust SSC* team brainstormed the worst things that could go wrong and made their plans from there.

For example, if one of the engines didn't work properly, special computer sensors were designed to notice the malfunction and reduce or shut off the power in the other engine. If the nose of the vehicle began to lift off the ground, a system was in place to increase the downforce on the nose. The system would then lift the rear portion of the car to provide greater downforce on the nose, while shutting off the engines and opening parachutes to stop the car very quickly, even at full speed.

Because the *Thrust SSC* was designed to travel so fast, vibration was a big concern. Vibration is a fast, shaking movement that can be caused by waves of sound bouncing off an object. Vibration on the *Thrust SSC* could be caused by the noise of the car echoing on the ground, by the engines, or by sound waves as Green traveled through the sound barrier. To protect the car's structure, the team built it from three different types of materials: carbon fiber, aluminum, and titanium.

Like any race car driver, Green wore protective gear to make sure he wasn't burned if there was a fire. Unlike most fire suits worn by race car drivers, though, Green's jumpsuit was made out of Panotex. This material offers more

FIRE SAFETY

In the event of a fire, the *Thrust SSC* team built several systems to extinguish the fire and protect the driver. Fire extinguishers were installed at points all over the vehicle and were designed to go off either by the driver's pushing a button, or automatically in the event of a crash. Special attention was paid to the cockpit, where driver Andy Green would sit. Sensors to detect changes in temperature were installed and connected to a warning light in the cockpit. Both fire extinguishers and a sprinkler system were designed to put out a fire in the cockpit.

protection than Nomex, the fabric used in most fire suits. Panotex looks a lot like cotton but repels liquid and protects the wearer at temperatures as high as 1,000°C (about 1,800°F). Green's helmet was also different from a race car driver's helmet. He needed to have an air supply to protect him in case of a fire or fumes in the cockpit, so he used an open-faced fighter pilot's helmet. The helmet included a mask that gave enough air to last 30 minutes. To protect his eyes, the sunglasses manufacturer Bollé designed a special set of goggles that would protect him even from a splash of molten metal.

With all the testing and precautions, Green was one of the best-protected drivers in the history of land speed racing. Yet none of the protective systems were used. Does that mean they were all a waste? No, absolutely not. Because of all of Green's training and all the testing that the *Thrust SSC* team did, they were able to achieve their goal of traveling faster than the speed of sound.

6

THE *INVADER* AND THE *EAGLE*

Noble, Green, and the rest of the *Thrust SSC* team reached their goal and set the new land speed record faster than the speed of sound. After this triumph, they decided they were done. The team members went back to their old jobs, and the *Thrust SSC* was stored in a hangar at Noble's company, Farnborough Aircraft. Although the British team moved on, other teams still continue land speed racing and have their sights set on a new record: 800 mph.

Rosco McGlashan is the owner and driver of the *Aussie Invader* team, based in Australia. A longtime racer, McGlashan currently holds the Australian land speed record, which was set at 498 mph in 1994. The vehicle he used was the *Aussie Invader 2,* a car with a design very similar to that of the *Thrust 2.* The team set the record at Lake Gairdner, a dry salt lakebed located in a very remote area of Australia. It is similar to the Bonneville Salt Flats of Utah, but Lake Gairdner is in excellent condition, with the salt surface as thick as four feet (about one meter) in certain spots.

Australia's land speed record holder, Rosco McGlashan, kneels next to the *Aussie II*. McGlashan attained a speed of 498 miles per hour in the *Aussie II* on the dry salt lakebed of Lake Gairdner in 1994.

A couple of years after his record, McGlashan traveled 643 mph in a new car, the *Aussie Invader 3*. A fourth car came next, but this jet-powered vehicle was not capable of traveling fast enough to set a new record. So McGlashan set out to build the *Aussie Invader 5R*, which was still in the developmental stages in 2007.

The *Aussie Invader 5R* will be 55 feet long and about 10 feet tall at its tallest point. It will be powered by two rocket motors that will be built by Space Dev of San Diego. That's the same company that built the motor for SpaceShipOne, the first plane owned by an individual, rather than a country, to fly into space. Each motor on the *Aussie Invader 5R* will be almost twice as powerful as the motors on the *Thrust SSC*. The Aussie team hopes that these motors can power the car up to a speed of 1,000 mph. One motor will propel the *Aussie Invader* up to 600 mph, and then McGlashan will turn on the second motor to give him enough of a push to set a new record. McGlashan hopes to have the vehicle ready to try for a new land speed record in late 2008.

AN AMERICAN TEAM TRIES AGAIN

Another team that hopes to set the next land speed record is the *North American Eagle*. This team has been working since 1994 to build a car that can compete for the world land speed record using the shell of a Lockheed F-104 airplane. At 56 feet long and weighing 13,000 pounds, the car looks much like the F-104 airplane with wheels.

The *North American Eagle* has five wheels. There are two in the rear, two under the middle of the vehicle, and one at the front. Because the *Eagle* is so long, the five wheels help make it more stable. When the team does test runs at slower than 350 mph, it uses a set of wheels with tires. At speeds faster 350 mph, the team switches to a set of wheels made from aluminum only, with no rubber tires.

The team is using a J-79 engine that has been tweaked for the job. This is the same kind of engine used in the F-104 airplane. The U.S. military has used this engine with a lot of success since 1956. It was also used in the B-58 Hustler and F-4 Phantom military airplanes. About one-third of the weight of the *North American Eagle* comes from the engine. It uses about 160 gallons of jet fuel every minute it is running at its top speed. The engine produces 55,000 horsepower.

Ed Shadle, co-owner and driver of the *North American Eagle*, works in the cockpit of the old jet body that he and co-owner Keith Zanghi converted into a supersonic contender for the land speed record.

To stop, the *North American Eagle* uses several special parachutes in combination with multiple braking systems. These parachutes are designed to slow the car down at a very high speed, and won't rip apart as they are opened. This technology might even be useful outside of land speed racing. Imagine what would happen if an airplane pilot knew that his plane was going to crash, and he could pull a lever that would release a giant parachute. Instead of crashing, the plane could lower to the ground more slowly, with a lot less damage.

Ed Shadle, the team's project manager, is also the driver for the *North American Eagle*. Every time Shadle climbs into the cockpit, he wears a fire suit and other racing gear to protect him if there is an accident or a fire. He has already piloted the vehicle on several low-speed test runs. For a land speed racer, that's faster than 300 mph. There will be many test runs, which will gradually increase in speed until Shadle and the team are ready to try to set a new world record. If everything goes as planned, the *North American Eagle* team will probably make their first record-setting attempt in the fall of 2008 at the Black Rock Desert.

On a test run in October 2005, Shadle drove the *North American Eagle* at 350 mph to test the steering, brakes, parachutes, and other devices. After several runs and some adjustments to the car, Shadle piloted the *North American Eagle* to a perfect run on a runway in Washington State. "It was like a Sunday drive, only much, much faster.

The *North American Eagle* comes to a rest after taking a test run on the El Mirage Dry Lakebed, located in the Mojave Desert in California. The use of rubber tires indicates the *Eagle* traveled at a rate of speed less than 350 miles per hour.

REINVENTING THE *EAGLE*

The body of the *North American Eagle* is an F-104 aircraft that was used by the United State Air Force from 1957 to 1970. This plane was used to test the J-79 engine and was later used as a chase airplane for the X-15 rocket-powered plane. It was flown by some of the most famous test pilots in history, including Chuck Yeager, who was the first person to break the sound barrier in an airplane. It was also flown by Space Shuttle Enterprise commander Joe Engle. *North American Eagle* co-owners Ed Shadle and Keith Zanghi bought the plane in 1998 without knowing its history. It was in very sad shape, with holes in its panels and lots of missing equipment. It wasn't until Shadle and Zanghi began to clean up the plane that they learned of its importance in American aviation.

It was similar to taking off and landing [in a jet] but without anything in between," Shadle said in an interview. A long-time racer and airplane pilot, Shadle said it is hard, even for him, to imagine driving at 800 mph.

Whether Shadle and the *North American Eagle* team can bring the world land speed record back to the United States is a question everyone in the sport is wondering. The car, the driver, the location, the weather, and many other factors all must to combine to be perfect. Just the same, Shadle and the American team aren't worried if the Australians or someone else sets the next record. After all, records have continued to be broken since the first one was set in 1898.

CHRONOLOGY

1898 Driving an electric car, Count Gaston de Chasseloup-Laubat of France sets the first land speed racing record at 39.24 mph.

1904 William Vanderbilt Jr. becomes the first American to set a land speed record on sand at a speed of 92.30 mph; the first record faster than 100 mph is set by France's Louis Rigolly at 103.55 mph.

1905 Daytona Beach, Florida, becomes the location of a world land speed record with Arthur MacDonald driving at 104.651 mph.

1927 Major Henry Seagrave of England breaks the 200-mph barrier on March 27, logging 203.792 mph in his car, the Sunbeam.

1935 Sir Malcolm Campbell drives his *Bluebird* at 301.129 mph on the Bonneville Salt Flats in Utah.

1963 In his car called the *Spirit of America*, Craig Breedlove sets a new world record of 407.447 mph on August 5.

1964 Breedlove and his *Spirit of America* break the 500-mph barrier on October 15, registering 526.277 mph.

1965 Breedlove sets a new world record at 600.601 mph on November 15.

1970 Croatian-American Gary Gabelich sets a new land speed record at 622.407 miles per hour, driving the *Blue Flame.*

1983 Richard Noble of England, driving the *Thrust 2,* takes back the land speed record for Great Britain, with a speed of 633.470 mph.

1997 Andy Green drives the *Thrust SSC* to a world record of 763.035 mph and breaks the sound barrier on land for the first time in history.

2005 Ed Shadle drives the *North American Eagle* in a successful low-speed test at 350 mph.

2007 Rosco McGlashan's *Aussie Invader 5R* is under development in Las Vegas, Nevada.

GLOSSARY

Aerodynamics—An area of science that studies the motion of air and the forces created around a moving object.

Downforce—Pressure directed downward, such as on a vehicle.

Hot rod—A car rebuilt or modified for high speed and fast acceleration.

Mach 1—The speed of sound. Ernst Mach, an Austrian physicist and philosopher, used this term to measure the speed of an object in relation to the speed of sound. Mach 2 is twice the speed of sound; Mach 3 is three times, and so on.

Rocket sled—A sled with rockets attached to it that, when fired, cause the sled to accelerate rapidly.

Shock wave—A wave of air formed when the speed of the object passing through the air exceeds the speed at which the air is traveling.

Sound barrier—A large, sudden increase in aerodynamic drag that occurs when a vehicle, such as an airplane, approaches the speed of sound.

Supersonic—Traveling faster than the speed of sound.

Velocity—The speed of an object.

Wind tunnel—A tunnellike passage through which air is blown at a known velocity to investigate air flow around an object (such as a car) placed in the passage.

BIBLIOGRAPHY

Breedlove, Craig, and Bill Neely. *Spirit of America: Winning the World's Land Speed Record*. Chicago: Henry Regnery, 1971.

Holthusen, Peter J.R. *The Fastest Men on Earth: 100 Years of the Land Speed Record*. Gloucestershire, England: Sutton Publishing, 2000.

Noble, Richard, and David Tremayne. *Thrust: Through the Sound Barrier*. London: Partridge, 1998.

Noeth, Louise Ann. *Bonneville Salt Flats*. Osceola, Wisc.: MBI Publishing, 1999.

Schleifer, Jay. *Bonneville! Quest for the Land Speed Record*. Englewood Cliffs, N.J.: Silver Burdett Press, 1995.

VIDEO

Extreme Land Speed—The Ultimate Race, Discovery Channel, March 2000.

Top Speed, History Channel, December 1999.

FURTHER READING

Hendrickson, Steve, and High Fleming. *Land Speed Racing (Motorcycles).* Mankato, Minn.: Capstone Press, 2000.

Holthusen, Peter J.R. *The Fastest Men on Earth: 100 Years of the Land Speed Record.* Gloucestershire, England: Sutton Publishing, 2000.

Jennings, Charles. *The Fast Set: Three Extraordinary Men and Their Race for the Land Speed Record.* London: Little, Brown, 2004.

Noble, Richard, and David Tremayne. *Thrust: Through the Sound Barrier.* London: Partridge, 1998.

Noeth, Louise Ann. *Bonneville: The Fastest Place on Earth.* Osceola, Wisc.: MBI Publishing, 2002.

Pearson, John. *Bluebird and the Dead Lake: The Classic Account of How Donald Campbell Broke the World Land Speed Record.* London: Aurum Press, 2002.

VIDEO

Extreme Land Speed—The Ultimate Race, Discovery Channel, March 2000.

Mega Builders: World's Fastest Wheels, Discovery Channel, January 2007.

Top Speed, History Channel, December 1999.

WEB SITES

www.aussieinvader.com
Official Web site of the *Aussie Invader 5R* team.

www.fia.com
The site of the Fédération International de l'Automobile, the group that oversees world land speed racing records.

www.landracing.com
Coverage of all types of land speed racing events, including current news on the sport.

www.landspeed.com
The official Web site of the *North American Eagle* team; includes history and general information on land speed racing and classroom resources.

www.racingcampbells.com
A Web site dedicated to Donald and Malcolm Campbell's land speed racing efforts.

www.saltflats.com
The online home of the Utah Salt Flats Racing Association.

www.scta-bni.org
The Web site for the Southern California Timing Association and Bonneville Nationals Inc., one of the groups that oversees land speed racing.

www.speedrecordclub.com
A Web site for all types of speed racing, on land, water, and air.

www.thrustssc.com
The official Web site for the *Thrust SSC* team.

PICTURE CREDITS

page:

8: © Getty Images
10: © AP Images
13: © AP Images
14: © Getty Images
18: © Bettmann/CORBIS
20: © AP Images
21: © AP Images
23: © Getty Images
25: © Bettmann/CORBIS
27: © Bettmann/CORBIS
29: © AP Images
31: © AP Images
33: © Bettmann/CORBIS
35: © AP Images
39: © AP Images
40: © Keith Kent/Photo Researchers, Inc.
42: © Getty Images
44: © AP Images
46: © AP Images
50: LandSpeed Productions
52: © AP Images
53: Photo by Tim Finley

Cover:
Andy Green sits on top of the jet *Thrust SCC* car before taking it for its first public test ride down the runway at Farnborough Airfield, near London, on October 14, 1996. (© AP Images/Max Nash)

INDEX

ABOUT THE AUTHOR

TARA BAUKUS MELLO is a freelance automotive writer. During her 20 years as a writer, she has published more than 3,700 articles in newspapers and magazines. Baukus Mello is the author of *Tony Stewart, Rusty Wallace, Mark Martin, The Pit Crew, Stunt Driving,* and *Danica Patrick,* all part of Chelsea House's RACE CAR LEGENDS: COLLECTOR'S EDITION series. A graduate of Harvard University, she lives in Southern California, where she cruises the streets in her 1932 Ford pickup street rod that she built with her father.